FN42

MICHELLE MAZZULO

SIQTDE

Vanity PL8
Puzzles

A Puzzle Book Where You Solve the Vanity Plates

Published by:
Santa Monica Press LLC
P.O. Box 1076
Santa Monica, CA 90406-1076
1-800-784-9553
www.santamonicapress.com
books@santamonicapress.com

SANTA
MONICA
PRESS

Printed in the United States

Santa Monica Press books are available at special quantity discounts when purchased in bulk by corporations, organizations, or groups. Please call our Special Sales department at 1-800-784-9553.

ISBN-13 978-1-59580-038-1
ISBN-10 1-59580-038-7

Library of Congress Cataloging-in-Publication Data

Mazzulo, Michelle.
  Vanity plate puzzles: a puzzle book where you solve the vanity plates / by Michelle Mazzulo.
    p. cm.
  ISBN 978-1-59580-038-1
1. Word games. 2. Automobile license plates—United States. I. Title.
  GV1507.W8M385 2008
  793.734—dc22

                         2008006727

Cover and interior design and production by cooldogdesign

Introduction

Vanity license plates have become a cultural phenomenon. You see them everywhere you drive, and the more you drive the more you become aware of their presence on the road. I challenged my friends and family with the puzzles in this book, and they soon found them to be so much fun that now they are obsessed with solving every vanity plate they see on the streets and highways. I think they all have a new favorite pastime!

Before you jump into trying to solve my vanity plate puzzles, I thought I'd present a bit of background on the actual plates themselves. Not many people realize that the U.S. government began issuing license plates as early as 1903. Massachusetts was actually the first state to manufacture them. They were originally made of iron and porcelain, but license plates have changed many times over the years. During times of war when metal was precious, they were made of leather-, wood- or even soybean-based fiberboard. Legend has it that these were very popular among goats, who would enjoy taking a bite out of them!

As with most cultural phenomena, there is a group of dedicated individuals who have turned license plates into a hobby. The Automobile License Plate Collectors Association, otherwise known as ALPCA (www.alpca.org), has over 3,000 members from 50 states and 19 countries who get together once a year at a national convention to buy, sell and trade license plates.

Here's a little trivia: Idaho was the first state to make a license plate with a graphic. And what do you think they placed on their plate? You guessed it—a potato! The most controversial state license plate is most likely New Hampshire's, whose slogan is "Live Free or Die." Onc couple challenged its use and the Supreme Court ruled the state could keep it, but citizens could cover it up on their license plate if they chose to do so.

As for vanity plates, Pennsylvania actually manufactured the first vanity plate in 1931. As Americans became more prosperous, vanity license plates became more popular. Presently, the state with the most vanity plates is Virginia; 16% of Virginia's registered vehicles sport one. This may be due to the fact that Virginia charges only a $10 fee when applying for the plate. On the other end of the spectrum, Texas has the fewest vanity plates; only .5% of their registered vehicles claim to have one.

Did you ever wonder if it is true that prisoners make license plates? Almost every state still uses prisoners as a labor force. This is actually considered a premier job in prison. The "tag plants" are self-sufficient, labor is cheap and it saves taxpayers' money. Prisoners earn a standard prison wage of 60 cents per day plus production bonuses of approximately $100 a month.

Today, there are approximately 9.3 million personalized plates in the United States. Some humor is intentional, such as "FN2B" ("Fun to Be"), and some is accidental. I read a story about a man entering his three choices for his personal plate. The first being "Boating," the second was "Sailing," and for the third he wrote "no plate" because if he couldn't have his first two choices, he wanted to forego his personal plate. Much to his surprise, he received his personal plate in the mail and it read "no plate." Within months, he received notice of 2,500 unpaid parking tickets from all over the state! Apparently when the police cite a car without a license plate, they write "no plate" and when this gentleman's new plate was entered into the system, it matched him up with all these citations. Imagine the chaos in his life!

People are so passionate about their chosen plate, that sometimes they are willing to get into a legal battle in order to obtain a specific plate or keep the one they already purchased. A man in Vermont has been battling for 2 ½ years to get a plate that reads "JN36TN" as this is a reference to John 3:16 in the Bible. A Utah woman won an appeal for "GAYSROK" and another woman in South Dakota has the DMV recalling her plate

"MPEACHW." Although plate requests go before a review committee, some do sneak through and occasionally have to be surrendered back to the state. This usually happens after someone has registered a complaint to the DMV that a plate is offensive.

There is a huge controversy over what can actually be printed on a plate and what is deemed inappropriate. Authorities do not allow any plates that are considered obscene, profane, inflammatory, or drug related. Many people claim the first amendment to the United States Constitution and its guarantee of "freedom of speech" protects their right to display whatever they choose to say, even when it's on a license plate. The government, however, insists that plates are a form of "government speech" since they are issued by a government agency, and therefore the first amendment does not apply to vanity plates.

Whatever side of the debate you are on, you can't deny that trying to solve vanity license plates is a great way to pass the time. I sincerely hope that you'll enjoy both the puzzles in this book and the ones you'll see on other automobiles while you're on the road. Have fun!

— Michelle Mazzulo

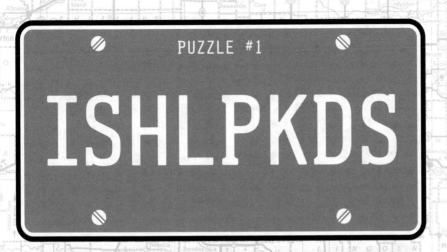

PUZZLE #1

ISHLPKDS

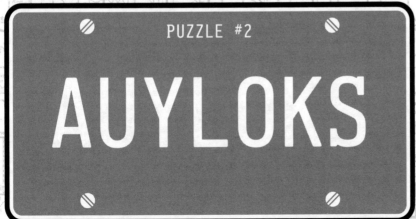

PUZZLE #2

AUYLOKS

Wyoming has had a bucking bronco on its plate since 1936 and his name is Steamboat.

Vanity PL8 Puzzles

Utah!—The only state to have an exclamation point after it.

PUZZLE #3

SIQTDE

PUZZLE #4

EZ2CYIO

Vanity PL8 Puzzles

PUZZLE #5

B4DKCME

PUZZLE #6

UEEEEA

Michigan has had
five different slogans
over the years.

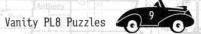

Vanity PL8 Puzzles

Arizona is the only state to use copper on its plates (1932, 1933 and 1934).

PUZZLE #7

TZVECL

PUZZLE #8

UNMLU

PUZZLE #9

PB4UGO

PUZZLE #10

RUNVUS

North Carolina and Ohio compete for bragging rights related to flight. Ohio's plates say "Birthplace of Aviation" and North Carolina's say "First in Flight."

Seventeen states still have their original slogans.

PUZZLE #11

TODALK

PUZZLE #12

OIOU2

PUZZLE #13

HIHOAG

PUZZLE #14

GRMPE

British Columbia produced black-and-white stickers for their plates but soon changed it to pink on white because people were making photocopies.

The last state to issue a statewide license plate was Florida in 1918.

PUZZLE #15

RATA2E

PUZZLE #16

2BENVD

14 Vanity PL8 Puzzles

PUZZLE #17

NTOTO2

PUZZLE #18

H8PEPZ

Some early plates had slits in them, allowing air to flow through so the radiator wouldn't be blocked and overheat.

There was a metal shortage for plates in WWII, thus some were made of wood.

PUZZLE #19

ML8ML8

PUZZLE #20

SGL4LIF

PUZZLE #21

XLR82XS

PUZZLE #22

GGGGGGG

In the 1970s, Utah's plate boasted a picture of a beehive.

 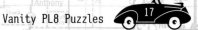

The University of Tennessee beat the University of Texas in the 1951 Cotton Bowl. The state produced that year's plate in UT's colors of orange and white, and these continue to be the most frequently sought after plates by Tennessee collectors.

PUZZLE #23

CNQRS8N

PUZZLE #24

IXFE

18

Vanity PL8 Puzzles

PUZZLE #25

LVIT2F8

PUZZLE #26

RIRUVRU

In Texas between 1907 and 1917, cars were registered by counties, with each county beginning with the number 1. There were over 200 counties and by 1917, there were over 200 cars with the number 1.

Idaho has a picture of a potato on it. In 1928, and again in 1948, it was a baked potato with melting butter.

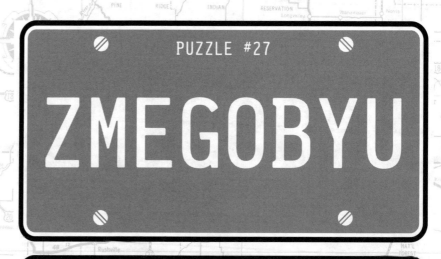

PUZZLE #27

ZMEGOBYU

PUZZLE #28

FUNCKER

PUZZLE #29

IM12XL

PUZZLE #30

IVARIVD

In Washington DC, the president was issued plate number 100 until the late '60s, when they stopped for security reasons.

Oklahoma boasted
a slogan that said
"Is OK!"

PUZZLE #31

2L82W8

PUZZLE #32

D8NNE1

22

Vanity PL8 Puzzles

PUZZLE #33

XKWIZIT

PUZZLE #34

SUR

In September of 1903, the state of Massachusetts began issuing what is generally accepted as the first state-issued license plate.

In 1916, the front tab for the California plate had a place for the owner to scratch in his or her name.

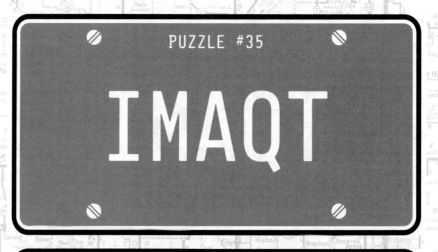

PUZZLE #35

IMAQT

PUZZLE #36

8ISEXC

Vanity PL8 Puzzles

24

PUZZLE #37

PAZAREV

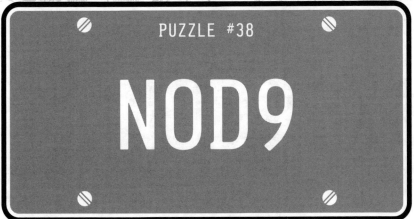

PUZZLE #38

NOD9

The 1941 Georgia plate was the first reflective state-issued license plate in United States history.

Vanity PL8 Puzzles

25

In 1992, New Jersey became the last state to switch to reflective license plates.

PUZZLE #39

CNTUCHDS

PUZZLE #40

SHRNNUF

PUZZLE #41

O2BNENG

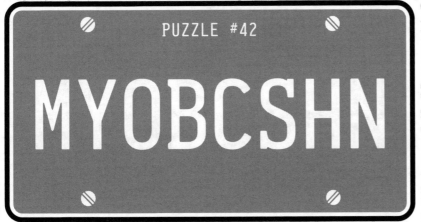

PUZZLE #42

MYOBCSHN

When quizzed, most people think Florida boasts the slogan "Vacationland"; however, it is the slogan of Maine.

The DMV has a "Blue List" of words or letter combinations deemed inappropriate.

PUZZLE #43

ATA2D

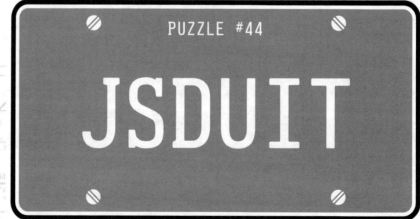

PUZZLE #44

JSDUIT

Vanity PL8 Puzzles

PUZZLE #45

IXCLR8

PUZZLE #46

2M80S

Vermont's slogan "Green Mountains" is actually redundant as Vermont is French for "Green Mountains."

A game show aired in the late '80s called *Bumper Stumper,* where contestants had to solve vanity license plates.

PUZZLE #47

ICI2I

PUZZLE #48

IDH82BU

30 Vanity PL8 Puzzles

PUZZLE #49

TI3VOM

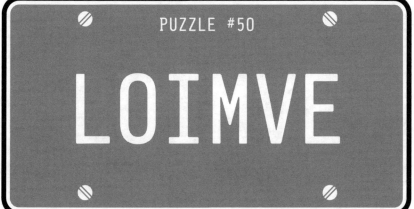

PUZZLE #50

LOIMVE

The highest reported price paid for a vanity plate was $14 million. The vanity plate "1" was bought at an auction in 2008.

 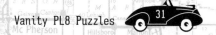

The DMV can recall a license plate at any time, no matter how long someone has owned it.

PUZZLE #51

HEBGBZ

PUZZLE #52

SOSUME

Vanity PL8 Puzzles

PUZZLE #53

UUUD444

PUZZLE #54

SEEADDS

Currently 32 states issue license plates in pairs. The other 18 issue a single plate for the rear of the car.

In the movie *License to Drive*, the license plate reads "GRANDPA."

PUZZLE #55

ITXLR8S

PUZZLE #56

AUDIGR

34 Vanity PL8 Puzzles

PUZZLE #57

OIMMI

PUZZLE #58

CUNOZ

The Yukon Territory preserves history with the slogan "The Klondike," named for the Gold Rush of 1896.

"Motu O Fiafiaga" means "Island of Paradise" and is the slogan on the plates in American Samoa.

PUZZLE #59

YY4U

PUZZLE #60

IH8WRK

PUZZLE #61

CTHRUU

PUZZLE #62

FN42

ALPCA is the largest organization of people interested in collecting license plates. The group was formed in 1954 and has a current membership of 3,000 people.

If you Google "vanity license plates," you can usually have over 800,000 websites to look through.

PUZZLE #63

CSTMIZ

PUZZLE #64

HEZIT8

38

Vanity PL8 Puzzles

PUZZLE #65

IMABZB

PUZZLE #66

CUL8RG8R

Wyoming is the only state to not have a slogan on its license plate.

President Roosevelt was the first president issued special plates in Washington DC for his inaugural parade in 1933.

PUZZLE #67

AXN28 D+

PUZZLE #68

MZLTF

40

Vanity PL8 Puzzles

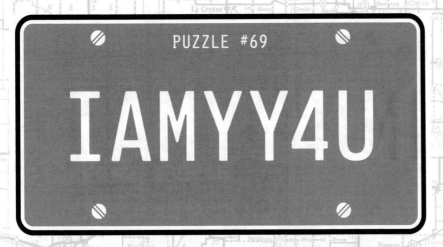

PUZZLE #69

IAMYY4U

PUZZLE #70

TOTLXTC

There was a contest in Canada to name the slogan for Saskatchewan's plate and lucky for them "Land of the Living Skies" won out. Other entries included "Eat Our Dust" and "Manitoba's Evil Twin."

Muhammad Ali was issued a plate with no numbers, just a picture of a boxing ring with two boxers.

Z3STUJZ

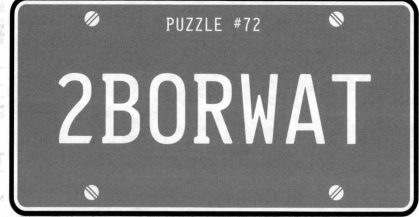

PUZZLE #72

2BORWAT

PUZZLE #73

NRG

PUZZLE #74

PHISHUN

Louisiana issued a plate in 1954 with a very simple slogan: "YAMS."

In many states, the number 1 is issued to the governor.

PUZZLE #75

PA2B

PUZZLE #76

CNTA4IT

44 Vanity PL8 Puzzles

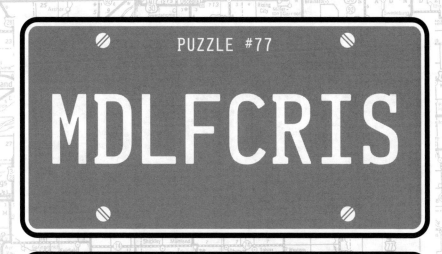

PUZZLE #77

MDLFCRIS

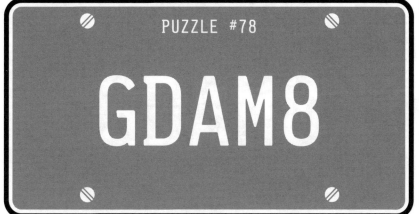

PUZZLE #78

GDAM8

You can ski in many states, but it is Utah's slogan that boasts "Greatest snow on earth!"

Many famous movies, including *Back to the Future*, showed vanity license plates. The plate for the DeLorean read "OUTATIME."

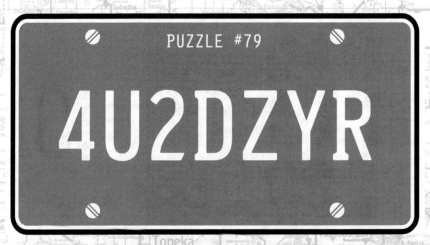

PUZZLE #79

4U2DZYR

PUZZLE #80

KMUNIK8

46

Vanity PL8 Puzzles

PUZZLE #81

RUD14ME

PUZZLE #82

24KTAU

California had a special optional plate made in 1984 celebrating the hosting of the Olympics. Naturally, it was red, white and blue.

Violinist David Rubinoff had a plate made with a picture of him playing a violin and the number 0.

PUZZLE #83

NVIGOR8

PUZZLE #84

DOOZPD

Vanity PL8 Puzzles

PUZZLE #85

O2BME

PUZZLE #86

GVML

In Nunavut, Canada, the license plate is shaped like a polar bear.

Florida issued the first Native-American tribal license plate.

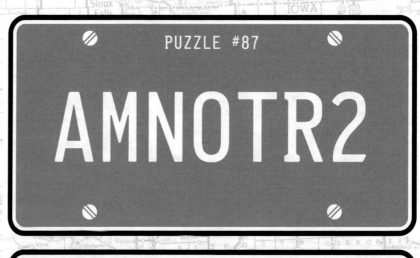

PUZZLE #87

AMNOTR2

PUZZLE #88

QTPA2T

50   Vanity PL8 Puzzles

PUZZLE #89

GO4THNX

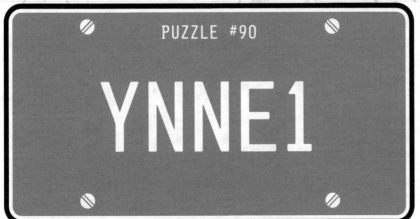

PUZZLE #90

YNNE1

The Yukon Territory license plate has a picture of a miner, commemorating the Gold Rush.

Pennsylvania was the first state to display a URL on the license plate: WWW.PA.STATE.US

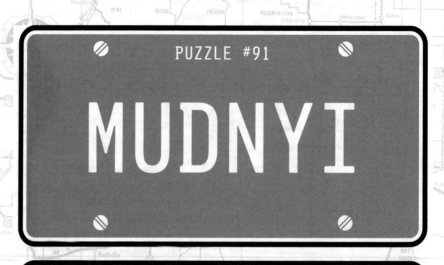

PUZZLE #91

MUDNYI

PUZZLE #92

GR82SH

52 Vanity PL8 Puzzles

PUZZLE #93

1DFOAL

PUZZLE #94

NEONE4T

One of the most coveted of all US-issued plates is from Alaska in 1921, as there are only a few known to exist.

Most states reserve the number 3 license plate for the secretary of state.

PUZZLE #95

8NOD9

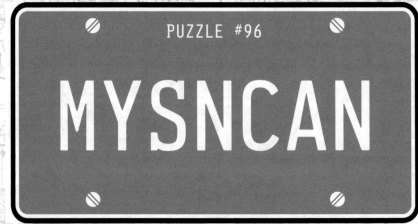

PUZZLE #96

MYSNCAN

Vanity PL8 Puzzles

PUZZLE #97

GN21OSE

PUZZLE #98

GR8D8B8

"GG-300" was the license plate on JFK's car when he was assassinated.

License plates varied from state to state and country to country until 1957, when government and international organizations came to an agreement on standardization.

PUZZLE #99

NIZ2CU

PUZZLE #100

IONU

56

Vanity PL8 Puzzles

PUZZLE #101

IW84NO1

PUZZLE #102

TXN4EVR

New Hampshire's slogan "Live Free or Die" is considered to be the most controversial slogan.

A standard license plate is 12 inches by 6 inches.

PUZZLE #103

YBNRML

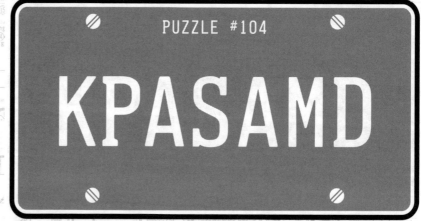

PUZZLE #104

KPASAMD

58 Vanity PL8 Puzzles

PUZZLE #105

2QCE465

PUZZLE #106

GURUGLY

The slogan on the Washington DC plates reads "Taxation without representation," which highlights DC's lack of voting power in Congress.

Causes including the Protection of the Sea Turtle are supported through special license plates and can earn over $1,000,000 a year.

PUZZLE #107

YY2MRY

PUZZLE #108

UCRED2

PUZZLE #109

1OSNE1

PUZZLE #110

NAHRTBT

Texans have to get new plates every 10 years.

On *Dukes of Hazzard*, Daisy Duke's license plate read "DIXIE."

PUZZLE #111

LVB4UDI

PUZZLE #112

14THBCH

Vanity PL8 Puzzles

PUZZLE #113

O2BNLA

PUZZLE #114

ICUCNME

License plates
were first called
"number plates."

Michigan makes about 2 million plates per year.

PUZZLE #115

I12BUGU

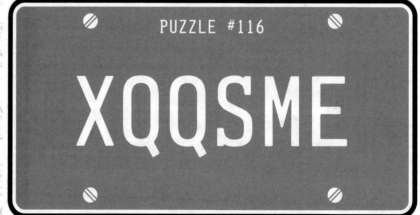

PUZZLE #116

XQQSME

Vanity PL8 Puzzles

PUZZLE #117

MPROM2

PUZZLE #118

IGOT2P

South Carolina used to have a slogan that read "The Iodine State."

In 2006, Wisconsin issued 178 plates for amateur radio enthusiasts.

PUZZLE #119

H8YNERS

PUZZLE #120

ICULAFN

PUZZLE #121

RMOTL6

PUZZLE #122

URNZWA

You can take your favorite plate and have a purse made out of it.

67

If 9 million license plates were recycled, it would produce 1,500 tons of aluminum.

PUZZLE #123

FNOMNL

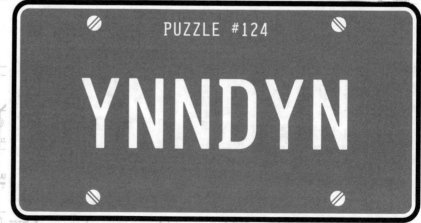

PUZZLE #124

YNNDYN

68 Vanity PL8 Puzzles

PUZZLE #125

MI3SUNZ

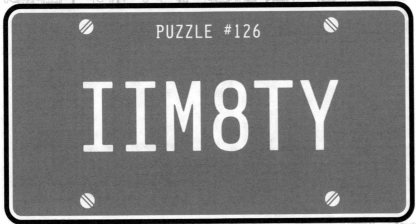

PUZZLE #126

IIM8TY

California license
plates in 1916 were
the first to be issued
with renewable
yearly tags.

 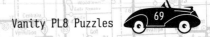

Idaho was the first state to bear a slogan: the 1928 "Idaho Potatoes."

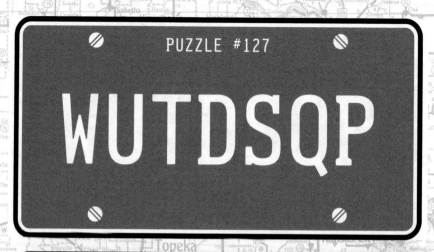

PUZZLE #127

WUTDSQP

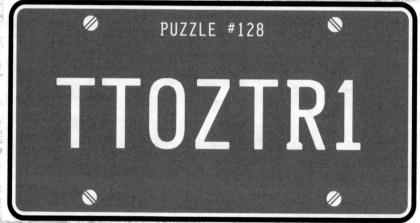

PUZZLE #128

TTOZTR1

Vanity PL8 Puzzles

PUZZLE #129

NS8IABL

PUZZLE #130

H2OMEN4

Kansas license plates were issued in a smaller size— almost as compact as a motorcycle license plate— to conserve metal during WWII.

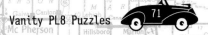

Arizona issued pure copper license plates in the 1930s to boost the state's copper industry.

PUZZLE #131

IH8PL8S

PUZZLE #132

W8N4FRI

PUZZLE #133

O2BCD8D

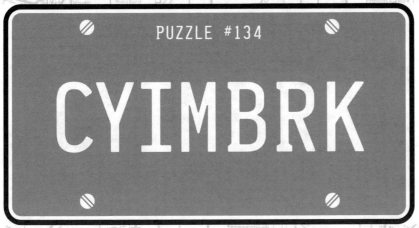

PUZZLE #134

CYIMBRK

Maine is the only state to use the full state name on every license plate it issues.

Montana license plates carried the slogan "Prison Made" for a number of years.

PUZZLE #135

XXRENUF

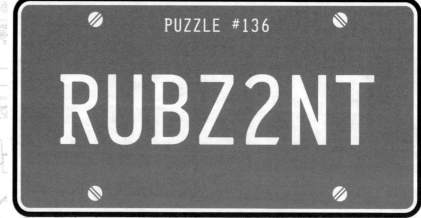

PUZZLE #136

RUBZ2NT

PUZZLE #137

12BL8

PUZZLE #138

IRIGHTI

With the exception of a couple of years, New Hampshire's plates have always been green and white.

In the beginning, New York put people's initials on license plates. Some argue these were the first vanity plates.

PUZZLE #139

BGNBD

PUZZLE #140

NT12WRK

76

Vanity PL8 Puzzles

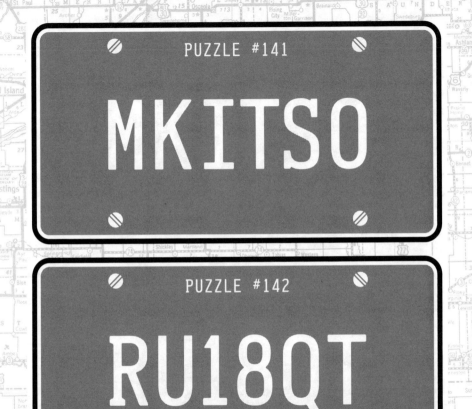

PUZZLE #141

MKITSO

PUZZLE #142

RU18QT

License plates for North Carolina came out in April of 1913. Legend has it that they expired June 30, 1913.

Vanity PL8 Puzzles

Rhode Island was America's second state to issue a license plate and for more than 80 years, it stuck with the black-and-white theme.

PUZZLE #143

ULIV1S

PUZZLE #144

IMGRJS

Vanity PL8 Puzzles

PUZZLE #145

BSTNSHO

PUZZLE #146

NE1CARE

From 1936 to 1956, Tennessee license plates were cut in the shape of the state.

Nebraska's first license plates were made out of leather.

PUZZLE #147

UBNPASD

PUZZLE #148

NLESRD

Vanity PL8 Puzzles

PUZZLE #149

IMARUNR

PUZZLE #150

CARPEPM

Vermont has almost 550,000 drivers and 32,000 of them have vanity plates.

"KNIGHT" was the license plate used in the TV series *Knight Rider*.

PUZZLE #151

KIDBGON

PUZZLE #152

BK2BA6

82 Vanity PL8 Puzzles

PUZZLE #153

RM41MR

PUZZLE #154

YYUUUU

A souvenir Winter Olympics plate would have been issued under an Alaskan Statute, but was repealed when Anchorage was not selected to host the Olympics.

Iowa, Minnesota and Ohio issue specially colored license plates to people convicted of DWI.

PUZZLE #155

UREBELU

PUZZLE #156

YUBSONOZ

Vanity PL8 Puzzles

PUZZLE #157

IMLEVNU

PUZZLE #158

CNTA4DU

In 1917, Colorado had a plate that was black on pink.

For a car to bear an antique automobile license plate, it has to be over 25 years old in most states.

PUZZLE #159

H2OUUP2

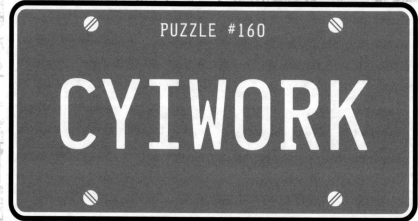

PUZZLE #160

CYIWORK

86 Vanity PL8 Puzzles

PUZZLE #161

B9S2US

PUZZLE #162

NJNEAR

There are almost 231 million licensed vehicles in the United States.

"USSC 102" is the license plate for Supreme Court Justice Sandra Day O'Connor, our 102nd appointed judge.

PUZZLE #163

NANYMIN

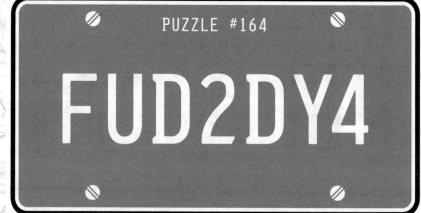

PUZZLE #164

FUD2DY4

Vanity PL8 Puzzles

PUZZLE #165

CYAH

PUZZLE #166

SCRMOM

One of Batman's license plates on his Batmobile was "BAT-1."

The most turned-down requests for plates include alcohol or anger.

PUZZLE #167

IN4CLAW

PUZZLE #168

HIOFSIR

90

Vanity PL8 Puzzles

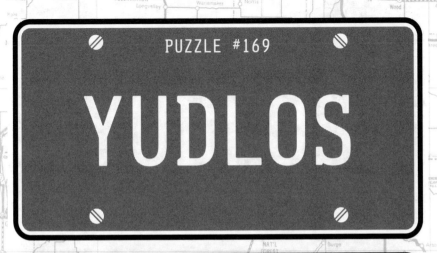

PUZZLE #169

YUDLOS

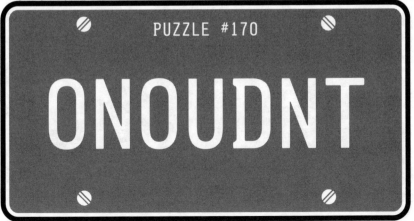

PUZZLE #170

ONOUDNT

In the 1960s, Arkansas's license plate read "LAND OF OPPORTUNITY." However, this slogan also appeared on plates from British Honduras (now Belize), as the plates were made by the same factory.

Alabama license plates were originally made of porcelain when they were first issued in the early 20th century.

PUZZLE #171

BZMOM

PUZZLE #172

GTCCRET?

Answers

1. ISHLPKDS—I schlep kids

2. AUYLOKS—Goldie Locks (Au=gold)

3. SIQTDE—Cutie (QT) inside

4. EZ2CYIO—Easy to see why I owe

5. B4DKCME—Before decay, see me (dentist)

6. UEEEEA—Euphoria

7. TZVECL—The 20/20 line on an eye chart

8. UNMLU—You animal, you

9. PB4UGO—Pee before you go

10. RUNVUS—Are you envious?

11. TODALK—To the lake

12. OIOU2—Oh, I owe you too

13. HIHOAG—Hi Ho Silver (Ag=silver)

14. GRMPE—Grumpy

15. RATA2E—Ratatouille

16. 2BENVD—To be envied

17. NTOTO2—And Toto too

18. H8PEPZ—Hate Pepsi

19. ML8ML8—I'm late! I'm late!

20. SGL4LIF—Single for life

21. XLR82XS—Accelerate to excess

22. GGGGGGG—G-string

23. CNQRS8N—Conquer Satan

24. IXFE—Nine iron (Fe=iron)

25. LVIT2F8—Leave it to fate

26. RIRUVRU—I love you (Scooby Doo)

27. ZMEGOBYU—See me go by you

28. FUNCKER—Fun seeker

29. IM12XL—I am one to excel

30. IVARIVD—I've arrived!

31. 2L82W8—Too late to wait

32. D8NNE1—Dating anyone?

33. XKWIZIT—Exquisite

34. SUR—Yes, you are

35. IMAQT—I am a cutie!

36. 8ISEXC—Ain't I sexy?

37. PAZAREV—Pa's a Reverend

38. NOD9—No denying

39. CNTUCHDS—Can't touch this

40. SHRNNUF—Sure enough

41. O2BNENG—Oh, to be in England

42. MYOBCSHN—My obsession

43. ATA2D—Attitude

44. JSDUIT—Just Do It!

45. IXCLR8—I accelerate

46. 2M8OS—Tomatoes

47. ICI2I—I see eye to eye

48. IDH82BU—I'd hate to be you

49. TI3VOM—Move it! (backwards)

50. LOIMVE—I'm in love! LO(I'm)VE

51. HEBGBZ—Heebie-jeebies

52. SOSUME—So sue me!

53. UUUD444—Use the Force (*Star Wars*)

54. SEEADDS—See a dentist

55. ITXLR8S—It accelerates

56. AUDIGR—Gold Digger (Au=gold)

57. OIMMI—Oh I am, am I?

58. CUNOZ—See you in Oz

59. YY4U—Too wise for you

60. IH8WRK—I hate work

61. CTHRUU—See through you

62. FN42—Fun for two

63. CSTMIZ—Customize

64. HEZIT8—Hesitate

65. IMABZB—I'm a busy bee

66. CUL8RG8R—See you later, gator!

67. AXN28 D+ —Accentuate the positive

68. MZLTF—Mazel Tov

69. IAMYY4U—I am too wise for you

70. TOTLXTC—Total ecstasy

71. Z3STUJZ—The 3 Stooges

72. 2BORWAT—To be or what?

73. NRG—Energy

74. PHISHUN—Fishing

75. PA2B—Father to be

76. CNTA4IT—Can't afford it

77. MDLFCRIS—Midlife crisis

78. GDAM8—Good day, mate!

79. 4U2DZYR—For you to desire

80. KMUNIK8—Communicate

81. RUD14ME—Are you the one for me?

82. 24KTAU—24 carat gold (Au=gold)

83. NVIGOR8—Invigorate

84. DOOZPD—Dues paid

85. O2BME—Oh, to be me!

86. GVML—Give 'em hell!

87. AMNOTR2—Am not! Are too!

88. QTPA2T—Cutie Patootie

89. GO4THNX—Go forth and multiply

90. YNNE1—Wine anyone?

91. MUDNYI—Mud in your eye

92. GR82SH—Great tush

93. 1DFOAL—Wonderful

94. NEONE4T—Anyone for tea?

95. 8NOD9—Ain't no denying

96. MYSNCAN—My tin can (Sn=tin)

97. GN210SE—Gone to Tennessee

98. GR8D8B8—Great date bait

99. NIZ2CU—Nice to see you

100. IONU—Eye on you

101. IW84NO1—I wait for no one

102. TXN4EVR—Texan forever

103. YBNRML—Why be normal?

104. KPASAMD—*Qué pasa*, Doc? (What's up, Doc?)

105. 2QCE465—Too queasy for 65 mph

106. GURUGLY—Gee, you're ugly!

107. YY2MRY—Too wise to marry

108. UCRED2—You see red, too?

109. 10SNE1—Tennis anyone?

110. NAHRTBT—In a heartbeat

111. LVB4UDI—Live before you die

112. 14THBCH—One for the beach

113. O2BNLA—Oh, to be in LA

114. ICUCNME—I see you seeing me

115. I12BUGU—I want to bug you

116. XQQSME—Excuse me!

117. MPROM2—Impromptu

118. IGOT2P—I gotta pee!

119. H8YNERS—Hate whiners!

120. ICULAFN—I see you laughing

121. RMOTL6—Our "Motel 6"

122. URNZWA—You are in the way!

123. FNOMNL—Phenomenal

124. YNNDYN—Wine and dine

125. MI3SUNZ—My 3 sons

126. IIM8TY—Aye, aye, matey!

127. WUTDSQP—What's the scoop?

128. TTOZTR1—Testosterone

129. NS8IABL—Insatiable

130. H2OMEN4—What are men for?

131. IH8PL8S—I hate plates

132. W8N4FRI—Waiting for Friday

133. O2BCD8D—Oh, to be sedated

134. CYIMBRK—See why I'm broke

135. XXRENUF—Two Ex's are enough

136. RUBZ2NT—Are you busy tonight?

137. 12BL8—One to be late

138. IRIGHTI—Right between the eyes

139. BGNBD—Big and bad

140. NT12WRK—Not one to work

141. MKITSO—Make it so

142. RU18QT—Are you 18, cutie?

143. ULIV1S—You live once!

144. IMGRJS—I am gorgeous

145. BSTNSHO—Best in Show

146. NE1CARE—Anyone care?

147. UBNPASD—You've been passed

148. NLESRD—Endless ride

149. IMARUNR—I am a runner

150. CARPEPM—Seize the night (Carpe=seize)

151. KIDBGON—Kid be gone!

152. BK2BA6—Back to basics

153. RM41MR—Room for one more

154. YYUUUU—Too wise for you

155. UREBELU—You rebel, you!

156. YUBSONOZ—Why you be so nosey?

157. IMLEVNU—I'm leaving you

158. CNTA4DU—Can't afford you

159. H2OUUP2—What are you up to?

160. CYIWORK—See why I work?

161. B9S2US—Be nice to us

162. NJNEAR—Engineer

163. NANYMIN—In a NY minute

164. FUD2DY4—Food to die for

165. CYAH—See ya

166. SCRMOM—Soccer mom

167. IN4CLAW—I enforce the law

168. HIOFSIR—Hi Officer

169. YUDLOS—You'd lose

170. ONOUDNT—Oh no you didn't

171. BZMOM—Busy mom

172. GTCCRET?—Got the Secret?